PRAISE FOR JUST LEAD

"Anton's book is a must-have addition to any leader's collection. Anton's 44 actions are succinct and practical yet highly impactful. I have had the privilege to personally see Anton deploy these masterful strategies and can attest to their effectiveness. I strongly suggest this book be mandatory for any leadership development program your organization embarks on."

-Darrick T. Paul, MBA, MHA, SPHR, SHRM-SCP, CPXP
Chief Human Resources Officer, former United States Army Reserve Officer, and former university associate professor

—

"*Just Lead* offers tangible strategies for mitigating the challenges in the present-day workplace. Anton Gunn graciously shares refined key tenets of leadership sure to upskill aspiring leaders and readers seeking to make a greater impact. This book will serve as your constant reference for guiding principles in the journey to cultivate high-yielding teams. Simply put, a RARE find!"

-Dr. Tiffany Victor, DNP, MSN, B.A., ACM-RN
Vice President Population Health and Care Management at Atrium Health

—

"This is a book I will keep by my side throughout my professional journey. Anton thoughtfully guides readers on a path of self-reflection through the 44 tips and concludes with action items crafted to keep everyone engaged. It's an easy read and conveniently organized for leaders to check in with themselves, especially when navigating challenging scenarios in the workplace."

-Nathalie Occean,
COO of MedHaul

—

"This book is a masterclass on servant leadership, and as usual, the wisdom and insight Anton Gunn shares are invaluable. *Just Lead* is a must-read for anyone looking to build or strengthen more diverse and inclusive high-performing teams in the workplace."

—Mia McLeod,
CEO of McLeod Butler Communications

—

"Thank you, Anton, for providing such concrete and practical tips that any healthcare leader could use to build the great teams we desperately need in healthcare. Our quality of care and leadership are critical to the health of our patients."

-Kimberly Butler Willis, Ph.D., CHES, CDP
SVP, Patient Care Operations; Planned Parenthood of Michigan

—

"Anton Gunn's insights demonstrate how to authentically break down barriers and overcome the challenges in law enforcement departments. You'll use these gems every day. The tips Anton shares in his book are critical to improving police culture and delivering positive results. It should be required reading for any law enforcement leader that wants to meet the challenge of diversity, equity, and inclusion in the post-George Floyd world."

—James A. Flowers, Jr.
CEO 431 Global, LLC

—

"Anton Gunn makes another content-rich contribution towards building a sustainable workplace culture with these 44 action steps. He is engaging and insightful and offers tangible techniques to implement immediately. *Just Lead* is a must-read for leaders at every level. It just makes sense!"

-Jerald Cosey
Operational Leadership Development Director
American Senior Communities

JUST LEAD

44 Actions to Break Down Barriers,
Boost Your Retention, and Build
a World-Class Culture

ANTON J. GUNN

Just Lead: 44 Actions to Break Down Barriers, Boost Your Retention, and Build a World-Class Culture

Copyright © 2022 by Anton J. Gunn

937 Strategy Group, LLC
www.937StrategyGroup.com

Book Creation & Design
DHBonner Virtual Solutions, LLC
www.dhbonner.net

ISBN for Paperback: 979-8-9866691-0-6
ISBN for eBook: 979-8-9866691-1-3

Printed in the United States of America

This book is dedicated to Kimberly Balaguer, Ronnie Chatterjee, Sarah de Barros, Stephen Graves, Frank Harris, Somayah McKinney, Chasity Ramos, Stephanie Taylor, Quenton Tompkins, Jean-Marc Villain, Antwan Walters, and Ashlynn Williams. Thank you for allowing me to *Just Lead* the best team ever.

Contents

ACKNOWLEDGMENTS

I must start by thanking my wife and life partner Tiffany Johnson-Gunn, and my daughter, Ashley. From listening to me on countless conference calls and video meetings to traveling with me and sitting in the audience as I brought these words and experiences to life, I am grateful for your active support of this book and my ministry to build a World-Class Workplace Culture®.

I want to thank my parents, Mona and Louge Gunn, who laid a foundation for my siblings and me to understand the importance of our family's legacy in service and empowering others. I want to thank my brothers Cherone, Jamal, Jason, and Keith. You have helped me to become a better leader. I needed you to become me. I also want to thank my extended family for giving me diverse and fantastic life experiences that helped me to understand and appreciate the world.

Thanks to everyone on our team who helped with this project. Regina Baker-Chenier, Desireé Harris-Bonner, and Kate Williams were instrumental to this book getting finished. Special thanks to Kim Balaguer and Stephen Graves. Your honest feedback and insights helped sharpen my thoughts, concepts, and stories into a blueprint for leadership and an action plan for cultural transformation. I truly appreciate our conversations and, most importantly, your interest in my work. Special thanks to Elle Petrillo and the Brand Builders Group Community for your thoughtful and impactful insights on this project. I am grateful.

To the phenomenal leaders I have had the privilege of serving under to hone and improve my skills: Myron Terry, Lenora Reese, John Ruoff, Arlene Andrews, John Niblock, Cassie Hahne Barber, Anita Floyd, Emma Myers, Teresa Arnold, Othello Poulard, Charlene Sinclair, Paul DioGuardi, Kathleen Sebelius, and Barack Obama... *thank you.*

I also want to offer special thanks to Antoinette & Walter Bond and AJ & Rory Vaden for their valuable coaching, mentorship, and friendship. Your transparency, honesty, and teamwork have changed my business. Thank you for being a part of my life and allowing me to be a part of yours.

Finally, I want to thank all of the employees, managers, directors, executives, and c-suite leaders who shared their professional and organizational challenges. The conception of this book would not have been possible without your real-life stories and experiences shaping the direction of this project. I would love to name each of you and your organizations, but the need for confidentiality and anonymity of many of the things you shared with me requires discretion. Just know that I saw what you went through, heard you, and gave my best strategy and insights to turn things around for you and others. Now, this book will be a living example of your experiences. Thank you for helping me provide other leaders and organizations with the solutions to prevent what you have endured.

INTRODUCTION

This is not your typical leadership book. It's short, direct, and to the point. This book is all about helping you to be a better leader right now. As you will quickly learn, we have some significant challenges in the American workplace. Resignations, lack of productivity, harassment cases, discrimination lawsuits, disengaged employees, and toxic workplace culture have spread like wildfire over the last decade.

These challenges are not only burning down our companies and industries; it is undermining American democracy. Some may think workplace issues and the stability of American democracy are unrelated, but they are the same. How we treat each other in society directly reflects how we treat people in the workplace. The way the public has lost trust and faith in our institutions is the same way people have lost faith in American employers.

Most business owners and company executives don't know how to address these challenges. In fact, they have allowed them to get worse. However, this book is going to provide a solution to these challenges. I am going to show you how to lead. More specifically, this book will give you a framework to create a world-class culture of justice in your organization. It intends to help leaders discover new ways to promote diversity, equity, inclusion, and trust in their work-places and teams.

If you are an experienced leader, this book should help you develop further as a leader to create positive change in your organization and ensure every employee is treated fairly and justly. It will also help you be a better leader for our society.

However, this book might not be for you if you are brand new to leadership.

At least, not yet.

Before you become a leader who can break down barri-ers, you must have some self-awareness and self-knowledge. In addition, you must know your "why" for leading. If your "why" is power, prestige, or control, you need to put this book down and consider reading my first two books: *Audacity of Leadership* and *Presidential Principles*.

This may mean devoting additional time to read and reflect on your purpose for leading people and teams. After all, there is a sacrifice involved in leadership. Think of some of the most admired leaders of our time – Martin Luther King Jr., Gandhi, and Nelson Mandela. They could only become legendary leaders because of their sacrifices for a greater purpose.

Compared to these leaders, giving up a little more of your time to read through books can help you reach a level of self-awareness as a leader so you can create a just workplace for you, your team, and your entire organization doesn't seem so bad, does it?

If you're not willing to take this first step of sacrifice, then maybe it's time to

> Before you become a leader who can break down barriers, you must have some self-awareness and self-knowledge. In addition, you must know your "why" for leading.

consider whether you're ready to be a leader. After all, there is a cost to instill healthy habits and become a just leader.

So why am I telling you how to lead? Because I need your help. We must rebuild trust in the American workplace. No one deserves to experience a lousy work environment. We need to fix it now, and I can't do it alone. We need more people to Just Lead.

And I fully understand this need because I have been leading at every level for twenty-five years — from small organizations with only four employees to large organizations with 80,000 employees — in private and public sectors, on college campuses, and in corporate corridors. I have helped organizations diversify their C-suite, improve employee retention and engagement, and trained more than 1600 physicians on diversity and inclusion leadership principles. Also, I have had the opportunity to provide leadership advice to CEOs, mayors, legislators, Congressmen, United States Senators, and even the President of the United States.

And, although I have won numerous leadership awards while mentoring hundreds, training thousands, and sharing my leadership principles with millions, it has always been my primary objective to leave people and organizations better than before, which is why I use and live by the actions highlighted in this book. Now, I want you to use these same actions to end the challenges others are experiencing in the workplace. Maybe you can help save our democracy by accepting your role as a world-class leader everyone will admire.

There is a sacrifice involved in leadership.

Defining Your Vision

Now that you have accepted your proper role as a leader and are ready to make some sacrifices, let's get started.

The first step to building a world-class culture is defining your vision. What do you want your culture to look like? How do you want it to feel when people enter your workspace?

Maybe you already have a vision and haven't figured out

how to make it a reality. Perhaps you don't even know where to start.

If you don't have a vision, don't worry. By the end of this book, you will know exactly what you need to do to get one. And if you have a vision but can't figure out how to implement it, this book will show you the steps you need to take to go from an idea to reality.

Of course, it's not enough to have a vision for what you want your company culture to look like and hope for the best. You also need to communicate it effectively to all levels of your organization.

I believe that effective communication is critical when casting and sharing a vision. You need to understand that everyone receives information differently. Your job is to know what's most important when communicating a vision. We should acknowledge that effective communication is written, verbal, and non-verbal.

Dr. Albert Mehrabian became famous for his research and theory on the 7%-38%-55% Rule for effective communication. This book is not to debate the science of efficacy of his study or rules; however, I use his theory to lay out my perspective on what it means for any leader that wants to break down barriers, boost retention, and build a world-class culture.

Effective communication involves three critical parts: your words, tone, and body language.

Your Words

Words are 7% of effective communication. If you want to connect with people, you have to choose the right words. Words matter! They can inspire and empower people, or they can make people angry. Using the right words is critical to painting a picture of your vision for a better culture.

Your Tone

Tone is 38% of effective communication. That's right; tone matters more than the words you choose!

When communicating your vision, you need to be confident and enthusiastic. You can't afford to be monotone, unenthusiastic, or unconfident. This goes for all types of communication. As a leader, you must always be aware of your tone, especially when communicating something negative. In that case, your tone may matter more than the actual words you use. The same is true for positive information.

Of course, it can be challenging to understand the tone in digital forms. When in doubt, communicate face to face instead of sending an email or text message with a tone that may be misinterpreted.

Your body language

The remaining 55% of effective communication is body language. This refers to your entire body, from head to toe. Body language communicates everything to the people you are leading. If you want to move people to change, you must use your whole body effectively.

That means you can't effectively communicate over text messages, email,

> The most inclusive leaders wake up every day intending to make the world a better place.

or phone conference calls. Instead, you need to go around to meet the people in your organization. If your company uses virtual meetings, keep your camera on and communicate your enthusiasm and commitment to your vision!

You can't make a change sitting behind your desk sending emails. Instead, you need to get out there and make personal connections with people in your organization, from top to bottom.

Prioritize Diversity, Equity, and Inclusion, and the Rest Will Follow

Every organization needs influential leaders. So, if you want to be the most effective leader possible, you need to develop a skillset and competency in the areas of diversity, equity and inclusion. The leaders who can do this will be the most significant impact players in an organization.

You win when you know how to lead a diverse team. Look at as many case studies as you want – the inclusive leaders who value diversity and surround themselves with various thoughts and demographics are the highest performers compared to their counterparts.

The most inclusive leaders wake up every day intending to make the world a better place. They recognize they are positioned to make the world a more just place for their employees and communities, regardless of what they may look like.

The most impactful leaders know they always have the opportunity to do something to make things better for all people. You might not be able to solve everything, but you can do small things to make it right.

You're not going to become a great leader overnight. So first, you need to reaffirm your purpose for leading. Then, you must accept that you still have much to learn about diversity, equity and inclusion.

If your "why" is power, prestige, or control, you need to put this book down and consider reading my first two books: Audacity of Leadership and Presidential Principles.

CHAPTER 1

PEOPLE
ARE FED UP

An estimated 38 million people have quit their jobs since 2020, with 24 million leaving in a short six-month span between April and September 2021.[1] Some are seeking employment elsewhere, while others have dropped out of the workforce altogether.

For example, a 2021 study from The Cengage Group found that 12% of people who had resigned from their jobs were not currently exploring new career opportunities.

This phenomenon of people quitting their jobs in droves during and after the COVID-19 pandemic is referred to as "The Great Resignation." And it's having lasting impacts on businesses in nearly every industry.

While some of the hardest-hit industries employ

---

[1] (*CG-great-resigners-research-report-FINAL.pdf* 2022)

blue-collar workers (e.g., retail, food service), The Great Resignation also affects white-collar workers, causing many to leave what seems like good, stable employment opportunities.

So, naturally, the question is, why are people so willing to leave their jobs, especially when they don't have another one lined up?

Several answers to this question depend on the employee and the company they are leaving. Yet they all boil down to one common theme – employees are fed up with being over-worked, underpaid, and underappreciated by companies who insist on putting profits over people.

Why So Many People Are Quitting Right Now

Mostly, there isn't just one thing that causes a person to leave their stable job. That's as true now as it has ever been. Instead, it's a culmination of several experiences that add up to an overwhelming desire to seek work elsewhere.

Let's take a closer look at some of these.

Toxic Work Culture

The average American spends more time at work than at home during any week. That's a lot of time to spend in an environment that isn't suitable.

MIT analyzed 34 million online employee profiles and found a toxic work culture to be the strongest predictor of industry attrition. Furthermore, work culture is so influential that it is ten times more important in predicting employee turnover than compensation.

"Company culture" is one of those buzz phrases people in human resources like to throw around in job descriptions and interviews. But what does it mean to have a toxic company culture?

Lack of Diversity

The MIT study found that failing to promote diversity, equity, and inclusion (DEI) was one of the leading elements contributing to toxic workplace culture. And yet, only 34%

of companies have enough resources to support DEI initiatives.[2] Furthermore, only 27% of companies understand how to measure the effectiveness of a DEI strategy.

Diversity applies to several factors, including race, class, gender, sexual orientation, age, and ability. Unfortunately, hiring managers often have implicit biases that keep them from hiring a diverse workforce, leaving employees who do not conform with the majority feeling left out and underrepresented.

Think about what you're doing for employees who represent diversity in the workplace: women, Black people, indigenous people, people with disabilities (or differing abilities), people from different ethnic or cultural backgrounds, and people who are older or younger than most of your workforce.

In addition to losing employees, your organization may face litigation if you don't prioritize diversity and inclusion. Every year, employers settle around $500 million in equal opportunity complaints. I don't want to see your name on a

---

[2] (*2022 workplace DEI report* 2022)

deposition or court document because you don't know how to hire and lead a diverse team.

High Turnover/Reorganization

Feeling engaged at work is difficult when you constantly worry about losing your job. It can also be demotivating to watch your workload double because a co-worker was laid off or sent to work on another team.

MIT found that employee turnover is higher among companies that frequently turn to reorganization and layoffs. These factors make it more likely that employees will negatively view their employers and be more likely to seek employment elsewhere.

Burnout/Exhaustion

There's a critical difference between working hard to get your job done and working so much that you cannot keep up with your normal activities. The latter is known as burnout, affecting more people than ever.

During the pandemic, healthcare workers, teachers, and hospitality workers suffered staggeringly from burnout. However, burnout is happening pretty much across the board. APA's 2021 Work and Well-being Survey found that 79% of employees were experiencing job-related stress.[3]

Additionally, 32% experienced emotional exhaustion, 36% reported cognitive weariness, and 44% of employees were physically exhausted. That last number is significant because it indicates a shocking 38% increase in physical fatigue among workers across industries since 2019.

Lack of Work-Life Balance

One leading cause of burnout is a lack of work-life balance. Many companies insist that employees work well past the standard 40-hour work week. The acceleration of digital tools for work (i.e., email, text, and mobile phones) can make it difficult for employees to feel like they fully get away from work. They're essentially "on-call" at all hours of the day and night.

During the pandemic, many people were forced to start

---

[3] (Abramson, *Burnout, and stress are everywhere* 2022)

working from home. They realized that they had more time in their day to focus on their families, their health, and other aspects of their lives. In addition, removing a commute and mindless chatter with office co-workers helped millions become more productive at work and more fulfilled in their personal lives.

Employees don't want to "grind" anymore. They've proven that they can be just as (if not more) effective when they have space to also focus on their personal lives. As a result, companies that demand employees to work long hours or commute to the office when they could just as efficiently work remotely are losing talented workers in droves. These employees are embracing the phenomenon known as "Quiet Quitting", a rejection of overwork culture.

Lack of Recognition

Employees don't necessarily need participation trophies; however, they enjoy it when their hard work and dedication to a company are rewarded. MIT found that employees are more likely to leave when their company fails to recognize and reward high performers.

While financial recognition (i.e., a raise or bonus) is appreciated, informal credit can go a long way. It can be as simple as a text message or email letting a team member know their work was recognized and appreciated. Knowing their efforts aren't going unnoticed helps employees stay motivated and engaged, leading to higher retention rates.

Lack of Opportunities

Companies with toxic cultures aren't the only ones losing talent amid The Great Resignation. Some companies may have a good or neutral culture but fail to provide the right opportunities to keep employees. Let's take a look at what some of those opportunities are.

Higher Pay

Naturally, compensation is a big deal, especially when we're in the middle of the highest inflation rates in over 30 years and are preparing for a seemingly inevitable recession.

A Pew Research study found that the number one reason

employees were leaving their jobs was because the pay was too low, which was reported by 63% of respondents.[4] Of these employees, over half (56%) said they were able to find a new job that paid more than the one they left.

A Lever study found a slight generational difference between those who would rather stay at a company that pays more versus businesses that provide a sense of purpose.[5] Between four generations (Baby Boomers, people born between 1946-1964; Gen X, born 1965-1976; Millennials born 1977-1994; and Gen Z, born 1995-2010), only two, Baby Boomers and Gen Z rated a sense of purpose as more significant than pay when choosing where to work. Millennials and Gen X overwhelmingly prioritize higher compensation over having a sense of organizational purpose.

Considering these generations will be in the workforce for the next several decades, companies should take notice and prioritize paying people what they're worth instead of getting away with paying employees as little as possible.

---

[4] (Parker & Horowitz, *Majority of workers who quit a job in 2021 cite low pay, no opportunities for advancement, feeling disrespected* 2022)

[5] (*The state of internal mobility and employee retention report* 2022)

Options for Career Advancement

Interestingly, the same percentage of respondents that said they were seeking employment elsewhere because of low pay also said they wanted more opportunities for career advancement.

Many workers have realized that they've gone as far as they can within an organization. With the retirement age steadily increasing, these employees are looking at working for at least five years longer than the previous generation before they can receive full retirement benefits.[6] So, why would they want to spend those years working somewhere that won't give them a chance to ever go beyond their current position?

Of course, sometimes, an employee simply outgrows their current company. This can be particularly true in smaller organizations with fewer options for people to advance into leadership roles. But, more often than not, there are options to promote current employees instead of hiring from the outside. Companies must shift their focus from constantly

---

[6] (*Social Security Fact Sheet*)

looking outward to figuring out how to advance current team members and promote from within.

Internal Mobility

While many want to advance in their careers, some employees want to switch roles without getting promoted.

A report from Lever found that 33% of employees don't feel like they can pursue a new internal role within their organization. Another 21% of employees don't think they can even approach the subject of seeking a new internal position with their manager, and 13% are unsure of whom to talk to about making an internal change within their organization.

The same study found that 61% of employees said they would search for a new role if their organization didn't allow them to make an internal change, and 67% said they would leave their organizations altogether if internal mobility were not an option.

These numbers demonstrate that employees don't necessarily want to leave their organizations to pursue new opportunities. Instead, they want to work for companies that will allow them to build knowledge and skills that can be used to pursue new opportunities as they grow in their field. More than that, they want to work with leaders who will help them identify options and help them build a career path that benefits them as individuals and the organization as a whole.

Yet they all boil down to one common theme: employees are fed up with being overworked, underpaid, and underappreciated by companies who insist on putting profits over people.

THE COST OF TOXIC WORKPLACE CULTURE

It is not a surprise that there are financial costs associated with recruitment. There are the costs to hire and retain a recruitment team, as well as costs associated with interviewing candidates and onboarding new employees. Some estimates put this cost at 150%-214% of an employee's salary.

However, the cost of not creating a just workplace culture to attract and retain talented individuals goes far beyond the initial costs of recruiting, interviewing, and hiring.

Financial Costs

In 2019, Gallup reported that employers pay anywhere from one-half to two times that employee's annual salary to replace them when an employee leaves.[7] That added up to $1 trillion for American businesses during pre-pandemic times. With more people leaving companies now than ever, these costs will quickly become burdensome for companies that have difficulty keeping people in critical roles.

The Society for Human Resource Management found that employers lost $223 billion because of toxic workplace culture due to turnover.[8] Organizations spend all their time recruiting talented people. But if they don't know how to lead a diverse team, the toxic environment can affect those talented people's performance and cause them to leave within one year of being hired.

Innovation Costs

Today's modern businesses thrive on innovation. However, employees who don't feel valued at work are less likely to share their innovative ideas. They may not want to risk

---

[7] (McFeely & Wigert, *This fixable problem costs U.S. businesses $1 trillion* 2022)
[8] (Hala, *The H.R. News Wire: Toxic Cultures have cost companies $223 billion over the last 5 years* 2021)

sharing a great idea just so an executive can claim the glory (and the financial compensation that goes with it). Or, they just might not care enough to put much effort into doing anything beyond their explicit job description.

Think about it. Can your business afford to function and grow without listening to and acting on the innovative ideas of your employees?

Loss of Institutional Knowledge Costs

In addition to all of the above costs, there are costs associated with losing company knowledge when an employee leaves. This cost, of course, gets higher the longer the employee has been with your organization.

It can be challenging to quantify the exact amount of money an organization loses when it loses an employee's knowledge. For example, consider how long it might take to find the answer to a question that a long-term employee would know off the top of their head. A new employee might spend hours, days even, trying to sort through the vast amount of information that has been dumped on their server to get close to the answer.

Relationship Costs

In addition to knowledge, employees who have been with an organization for a long time take the relationships they have built with them. These can include internal relationships as well as partnerships with vendors, suppliers, and possibly even clients. Losing one employee can set a business back significantly if they have to start over by building new relationships and partnerships.

Productivity Costs

Losing one person on a team may not lead to much extra work, particularly for large groups. However, losing 21 or more employees in less than a year (which happened to 12% of companies in 2021) means there's more work to be done by fewer people.[9]

---

[9] (Patel, *Gauging the impact of the great resignation* 2022)

It's hard to be productive when you're doing the work of one and a half people. But, more importantly, it's nearly impossible to think about growing a business when your entire staff is struggling just to stay above water. Thus, your organization cannot reach its full productivity potential when so many vacancies exist.

Once you add up all the costs of losing employees (financial and otherwise), you can see that there may be benefits to putting the time and effort into building a healthy work environment.

Losing one employee can set a business back significantly if they have to start over by building new relationships and partnerships.

THE PAYOFFS OF A WORLD-CLASS WORKPLACE CULTURE

In the same way that employee attrition costs far more than dollars and cents, the benefits of taking steps to create a great culture will reward your organization beyond its finances.

Being a good leader means having a strong team that will support you in every aspect of your personal and professional journey. It also means helping your organization stem the tide of talented employees leaving to work for your competition because they feel the culture is toxic. Let's walk through some of the payoffs businesses experience once their leaders put the work into building a great culture.

Higher Employee Retention

The statistics I've quoted don't paint a pretty picture for employee retention, at least not among companies with toxic cultures.

However, we're not seeing 100% of employees leaving their jobs. Many people stay right where they are if they are already working where they feel valued. That means they have a healthy work-life balance, reasonable compensation, and opportunities for advancement.

Just as it costs a company money to recruit and hire a new employee, it costs job candidates a lot of time, money, and resources to look for a new job.

> Bottom line: Employees who already feel valued and appreciated don't have an incentive to go into a flooded job market.

More Engaged Employees

It's no secret that employees who don't want to be at work tend to be unengaged. They show up daily with one goal–to do their job and collect their paycheck. As a result, they don't care about helping your organization grow into new markets, expand into a new set of services, or build a world-class reputation.

On the other hand, engaged employees are the ones who will develop new, innovative solutions and work hard to meet your company's goals. One study found that engaged employees can lead to a 202 percent increase in productivity.[10]

And here's the thing – you don't need to make a monumental effort to see some of that increase (although, of course, you might need to if you want to reap all the benefits of having a healthy culture). The same study found that 69% of employees said they would work harder if recognized for their efforts.

> Bottom line: Getting more engaged employees is as simple as recognizing their hard work.

Higher Performing Teams

In addition to getting individual team members to work together, you'll be able to get different teams to collaborate, which can lead to innovative breakthroughs that take your business to the next level.

---

[10] (*Employee engagement statistics 2022: Increased productivity?* 2022)

Of course, all this innovation and collaboration will impact your bottom line, making your business more profitable than ever because your employees are giving it 110 percent every single day.

> Bottom line: When your employees are more engaged, your teams can work together more cohesively to deliver better results.

Better Reputation

Today's job-seekers can have their pick of roles. They won't want to waste time on a company with a toxic culture. In fact, 86% of job seekers actively avoid applying for positions at companies with a bad reputation.[11]

> Bottom line: Your organization will struggle to find and hire talented workers until you fix its culture.

---

[11] (*Employee engagement statistics 2022: Increased productivity?* 2022)

Personal Influence and Success

By prioritizing a healthy work culture, you will build your influence and reputation as a leader in your space. This can open up investment partnerships, speaking engagements, thought leadership opportunities, and more.

> Bottom line: Your personal brand can only be as successful as your company. If you choose to maintain a toxic culture, you will never be able to grow beyond your current status.

I like to say that culture changes at the speed of trust.

THE PROCESS OF DEVELOPING A WORLD-CLASS WORKPLACE CULTURE

So, how do you go about building a world-class culture within your organization?

I'll get into more details in the next section with 44 actionable steps you can take starting today to do just that. But, first, I want to start with three questions every employee wants to know, whether they speak it or not:

1. Do you care about me?
2. Will you help me [to be successful]?
3. Can I trust you?

These are the three questions employees are trying to answer at every step of the recruitment, hiring, and retention process. They start asking these questions before applying for a position at your company and continue asking them every day before they come to work.

With The Great Resignation, it's becoming clear that employees aren't accepting "no" as the answer to any of those questions.

Let's break these questions down a little more to talk about what employees want to know and how you, as a leader, can give them the answer they're looking for.

Question 1: Do You Care About Me?

We all want to belong to a community, a team, and a world that accepts us for who we are and has our back. We don't want to be left alone or deemed a loner. Nothing good comes from being a loner.

So, as a leader, you need to identify whether you have loners on your team. You very well might. That's not a bad thing, inherently. However, if you do, you must demonstrate that you care about them, so they don't stay alone.

The reasons we discussed in Chapter 1 are why it matters that you find answers to this question. If an employee does not feel valued because they are paid too little money, are disrespected, are not given opportunities to advance, or are burnt out, they will answer "no" to this.

So, how can you turn that "no" into a yes?

It starts by serving your people. You have to care about your employees and their well-being. Instead of viewing employees as resources to suit your needs, think about how you can serve them.

How do you show them you care? It starts by demonstrating that what's important to them is also important to you. In chapter five, I'll walk you through a series of questions you can ask each team member to learn about what they value. Of course, understanding what's important is only one part of the equation. To truly demonstrate that you care about someone, you need to apply what you learn from your team members to inspire and empower the organization.

Question 2: Will You Help Me?

In addition to belonging to a community, we all want to succeed at work. Nobody is walking into the office every day, hoping to fail.

That's why employees look to their leaders to help. Your team should feel like you are willing to help them do their jobs better.

Employees want to know they can turn to their leaders when they need help with something, whether it's learning a new skill, getting access to new tools, or getting some relief as they approach burnout.

For example, a recent report from Deloitte found that the top driver of burnout among workplace employees is a lack of recognition and support from the leadership team.[12] This lack of support and acknowledgment can lead employees to work longer hours, take fewer vacation days, and feel more reluctant to ask for help when needed.

As a leader, you are responsible for giving your team members the tools, information, and resources they need to be well-equipped to do their job. The question for you is, "what are the tools your team needs to succeed?" As a follow-up, "what's standing in their way of getting them?" As a leader, you need to do whatever it takes to break down whatever barriers are standing in the way of your team and

---

[12] (*Workplace Burnout Survey: Deloitte Us* 2020)

the tools they need so they can excel at their jobs. You have to show your team that you want to help them.

Question 3: Can I Trust You?

I like to say that culture changes at the speed of trust. The greater your confidence in an organization, the more significant your cultural change.

Trust is hard to gain and easy to be broken. So, as a leader, you need to ask yourself a few questions:

- Am I trustworthy?
- What am I doing to show my team that I trust them?
- How do I build trust among my team by standing up for them to other leaders?

Trust is essential in determining how successful an employee will be at their job and how likely they are to stick around.

According to the Harvard Business Review, employees who work in trustworthy environments are better than those who don't work in high-trust companies.[13] They tend to collaborate more with colleagues, have higher energy, and have higher retention rates. In addition, they have happier personal lives and are less likely to deal with chronic stress.

And yet, one in three people don't trust their employer.[14]

When there is a lack of trust in the workplace, productivity and innovation are lost. Thus, to answer this question, you need to become a trusted leader. You can't be throwing your team under the bus or calling them out in front of senior leaders.

Instead, you need to demonstrate to your people that you care about them and are willing to help them (more on this in the next section). Once you have shown those two things, your team can start trusting you.

---

[13] (Zak, *The Neuroscience of Trust* 2021)

[14] (Ladika, *Trust has never been more important* 2021)

By serving me, she taught me to serve others.

44 ACTIONABLE STEPS TO BUILDING YOUR WORLD-CLASS CULTURE

CHAPTER

5

As a leader, you want to get off to a good start. If you don't, your team won't have any confidence in you. Further, they'll lose faith that you deserve to be in a leadership position. When that happens, your team will start coming up with their own ideas and go around you. They might get fed up and say, "Why should I work for someone who doesn't have the competency to lead?" And they'll leave, just like that.

I don't want that to happen to you. So instead, I want you to walk into a leadership position confident that you can lead your team and take them where they need to go.

That's going to take some work. But don't worry, I've got you covered.

In this chapter, I'll go through 44 actionable steps you can take starting today to build a world-class culture that values employees and attracts the most talented people in your industry. By implementing these 44 actions into your culture, you'll have your pick of the most gifted people in the world ready to help you build and grow your business.

I've divided the 44 actionable steps into three main categories: Service, Empowerment, and Legacy.

PART 1:
Service is the prerequisite of leadership

You cannot be an effective leader until you commit yourself to acting as a servant to those you lead. The best leaders do not insist on a "my way or the highway" approach. Instead, they value getting input from others, especially when that input is different from traditional ways of thinking. In addition, world-class leaders genuinely care about the people they lead.

Here are 12 ways to show your team that you care about them. You need to fulfill these before you can move forward. Take your time and put everything into it. Once you have successfully made these steps a regular habit, you can empower your team and earn their trust.

Remember, you can't change the culture of your team without changing your relationship with each team member.

01 Get to Know Your Employees Individually

No matter how large your team grows, it's essential to remember that it is made up of individual people who bring their unique backgrounds and experiences to the table. Everyone in your company has a story. That's why it's so important to get to know everyone on your team as people, not just employees.

You should have an understanding of what motivates them. You should learn what they are proud of and how they hope to develop in their careers. Beyond their career goals, you should understand their life goals. Remember, you can't change the culture of your team without changing your relationship with each team member. Learn what inspires them and what frustrates them.

02 Be Curious About Their Life Story and Journey

Don't just hear what your employees tell you; genuinely express interest in their stories and experiences! Ask questions as they tell you about their journey. You'll be surprised at the incredible things you can learn from someone by asking the right questions. Here are five questions I ask every employee that has worked under my leadership.

Where did you grow up? Understanding where a person grew up can tell you a lot about how they see the world. For instance, someone who grew up in the rural countryside will take a different approach than someone who grew up in a city. The same goes for someone who grew up in a different state or country. On the other hand, maybe you grew up in the same area and have shared connections. This question is the starting point for learning more about your team member's perspectives.

What's the best gift that you've ever been given? This question will allow them to think back through their lives about the most meaningful thing someone gave to them. Be careful not to specify gifts (e.g., Christmas, birthday, etc.). Their answer might not be a gift in the traditional sense. For example, maybe they were recognized as "Employee of the Month" for the organization, making them feel like they were a significant contributor. Whatever it is, the answer to this question can give you insight into what you can do to show your employee that you care about them.

What's the best part about your job? We all have things we love and hate about our jobs. However, we often focus on what we dislike more than what we like. When you ask someone to tell you what they love about their job, you will get insight into what's important to them. This can help you identify opportunities for them to contribute in ways that will help the organization and make them happy.

Why do you choose to work here? Every day, your employees wake up and decide to come to work. So, the answer to this question helps you learn what motivates a person to go to work every day. What is it about this organization specifically that gets them excited? Maybe it's you as their leader or the particular tasks they do every day. Or maybe they're working for the pay and benefits. Perhaps they need health insurance or like that the office is located close to their family.

There are all kinds of reasons. None of these reasons are for you to judge your employees but to gain an understanding of the person you lead. Besides, knowing why your team members chose to work here with you will help you learn what motivates them.

If you were in charge for a day, what's one thing you would do to change our organization and make it better? This question needs to come from you, a leader because you are the person the employee looks up to. As such, you are the one who can do something about it! Hearing the answer aloud lets your team members tell you about their number one source of frustration.

03 Check Your Bias

It is an unfortunate truth that we all have biases. Yes, even you. It's critical to acknowledge what those are so you can take steps to lessen biases that could have harmful effects on your team. We often think of bias as discrimination regarding gender and race, but it can also extend to age, geography, education, class, and disability. Never count somebody out just because you are predisposed to think of them in a certain way.

You need to self-reflect and be self-aware of your own biases before you start listening to other people's stories. Once you have given your bias some reflection, you'll be better prepared to know where your judgment comes in when you talk to someone.

Then, you can intentionally seek the opinions and perspectives of people who are different from you or disagree with you. For example, do you know that person who constantly contradicts your ideas? Instead of writing them off entirely, take that person out for coffee and get to know them. Listen to where they are coming from. There's a good chance you have more in common than you think. And who knows? They might even change your mind and push you to become a better leader.

> It is an unfortunate truth that we all have biases.

04 Commit to Serving Your People Before You Try to Lead Them

When you commit to a service mindset, you will be rewarded more than you can imagine. Being a servant means doing whatever it takes to help your team deliver.

So, rather than asking your team what they can do for you, find out what you can do for them. What can you do to make their jobs easier? What do they need to be successful? Resources? Training? Time? Collaboration with other teams? More money? Focus on doing what it takes to allow your team to shine.

05 Solve Their Daily Problems

Leaders often take more of a big-picture approach than small details. But that can be a mistake when you're leading a team. So, don't write off the problems your team comes to you with that seem minor.

For example, you might not think the broken coffee maker in the break room is a big deal. But your employees who rely on that for their morning pick-me-up might have to either leave the office to buy coffee or get some on their way in. That can mean getting up earlier, fighting traffic, and paying extra money for something that's usually a work perk. Their day is already off to a bad start, and they haven't even begun working yet. A second example could be the team member who works remotely but struggles every day because their work laptop reboots three to four times a day, and they lose sixty minutes in the work day starting over. Yet, no one at the company I.T. Help Desk is willing to just replace the laptop without approval from three different people.

06 Meet With Them One-on-One

Team meetings ensure everyone is aligned with your company and team mission. However, one-on-one meetings are the best way to get to know each team member and find out what they need from you.

Often, team members who are quiet during team meetings have great ideas; they might be uncomfortable speaking up in front of a group. So, one-on-one time with them is an excellent way to hear their thoughts and discover what they need from you to succeed.

These one-on-one meetings should be at least 30-minutes

each. Through these meetings, you'll learn what each individual wants in company culture, so you can work together to build the kind of culture that supports their needs and allows the organization to thrive.

One important note: your team members may share personal information with you in one-on-one meetings, especially once they trust you. To keep their trust, it's essential that you must not use anything they share with you in a negative way or in a way that embarrasses them. Instead, use that information in an inspiring and empowering way to build them up.

07 Actively Listen to What They Share With You

Don't think of one-on-one meetings as checking off a box. Instead, listen to everything your employees share with you. Keep distractions outside of the meeting. That means turning off your notifications and leaving your laptop behind. Focus entirely on what your team members have to say.

I call one-on-one meetings "journalism meetings." Think about what you would do if you were a journalist for a national magazine with the opportunity to interview one of the world's most famous people for a feature article.

Would you walk into that meeting without preparation and assume you could ask questions on the fly? Of course not! You would take time before the meeting to thoughtfully prepare questions that would offer insightful details about the person that you could connect to your audience of readers. Give your team members the same respect a reputable journalist gives a celebrity.

Now, it's essential to know that your team members will be able to recognize whether you are genuinely interested in what they have to say or are just asking questions to fill up a thirty-minute timeslot. If you are not ready to listen, don't try to operationalize this action until you have completed actions 1–3.

08 Learn What's Important to Them

If you want your team to help you build a better culture, you need to connect with them on a deeper level. And to do that, you need to find out what matters to them personally and professionally.

Use your one-on-one meetings to find out what motivates your team. Find out what they value. This will allow you to identify the key projects and opportunities that excite them and push them to excel.

09 Understand and Empathize With Their Perspective

You will encounter people with different ideologies and philosophies from you. As a leader, you need to accept this. More than that, you need to embrace it.

You can be empathetic even if you don't agree with everything an employee believes. Showing empathy as a leader will build trust with your team. They will know they can come to you with their problems and concerns and that you will not ridicule or minimize them. This type of trust is what separates adequate leaders from exceptional leaders.

10 Build Their Confidence

It can be difficult for people to recognize their strengths, so your leadership must build confidence as your employees grow in their roles. Offer praise at least as often as you give criticism. In addition, celebrate every win, no matter how small it might seem. Share success stories with the rest of the team and the company as it makes sense.

11 Be an Ally When They Experience Unfairness or Injustice

As a leader, you serve as your team's voice, especially when they experience unfairness or injustice in the workplace. You need to have their back. Don't "throw them under the bus" to other leaders, no matter what mistake they may have made.

After going through actions 1–10 above, you should know your people. So, don't let other people's lack of knowledge or insecurity about the people on your team affect your perspective. Some ways to be an ally include:

- Standing up for DEI practices
- Creating diversity initiatives if they don't exist
- Speaking up when you witness injustice in the workplace
- Recognizing your privilege and using it to be a voice for your team
- Facilitating inclusive meetings that ensure everyone in the room has the space, opportunity, and support from you to speak up

As a leader, you are responsible for letting your team know how they are performing – the good, the bad, and the ugly...

12 Invest in Their Personal Development (i.e., Essential Skills)

We hear a lot about soft skills being the missing link when it comes to professional development. The term "soft" refers to things like attitude, emotional intelligence, growth mindset, being a team player, openness to feedback, and work ethic. These skills are not soft — they are critical. They are critical to success in the workplace, but more importantly, they are essential for personal growth. You should invest in your people's personal development.

Some ways to promote personal development in your workplace include:

- Starting a book club
- Encouraging mentorship
- Doing team-building exercises
- Encouraging knowledge sharing
- Having employees set individual goals
- Modeling the behavior you want to see

Lastly, let's stop referring to these skills as "soft" and call them essential.

CASE STUDY: LENORA'S LEADERSHIP

My first full-time job after college was working for a nonprofit organization. I had no meaningful work experience to qualify me for the job. I majored in history and had never worked in public policy or health care. What I did have was a passion for justice and equity.

My boss, Lenora Bush Reese, also had a passion for justice and equity. By living the first twelve actions in this book, Lenora would change my life forever.

As the chief executive of a nonprofit, Lenora had lots of responsibilities. She was responsible for raising the money, managing the money, setting organizational policies, training the staff, and being the chief spokesperson for the organization. This was the job. However, she would share with me many years later that her most important job was to invest in and develop me as a leader.

She inspired me every day as I watched how she worked with people and how she shared herself and her expertise. Lenora Bush Reese remains one of the most important mentors of my life. Lenora empowered me by helping me develop the tools I would need to succeed. Not only did she believe in my success, but she also wanted those we served to be successful.

Nearly immediately upon hiring me, she poured out her personal contacts and relationship for me. She introduced me to every friend and colleague she knew who could be helpful to me in doing the job she had hired me to do. She took me under her wing, trained me, mentored me, and taught me the skills I needed to be a successful professional. I learned more working with her in the first few months than some people learn in a lifetime.

One of the most powerful things about Lenora was that she would ask me questions about me and not just about work. She always made it clear she was just as interested in me as she was in the job I was doing, in part because doing so helped me do the job better. She asked about my personal interests, my family, and my goals. Lenora also made it clear that I should never be afraid to ask her a question, and she never thought it was a problem to take time to answer my questions or teach me the nuances of policy or demonstrate ways to reach out to the community.

She taught me to read the editorial pages of the newspapers, specifically the letters to the editor, for by doing so, I quickly learned what was on the minds of community members and knew where to start a conversation. She provided me opportunities to learn, even going so far as to encourage me to apply for national leadership development programs. She was constantly teaching me and providing me with resources to learn from.

Lenora didn't stop at teaching me about public policy and health care; she taught me how to be a leader, how to engage more deeply with anyone I spoke with, and how to serve others. She equipped me through experience and through her knowledge of what I needed to be effective. By serving me, she taught me to serve others.

Lenora created one opportunity after another for me. Despite investing heavily in me through

> People expect a leader to take them to new heights, but they also expect a leader to be connected to the reality of where they have come from.

generously sharing her time and knowledge, when she saw opportunities for me to advance my career and increase my paycheck, she took action. At one point, she handed me a job announcement for another nonprofit. With her encouragement, I applied for the job, and when they called to check my references, Lenora told them I was making $25,000, and the only way they would get me was to pay me $30,000. I was making $19,000. Lenora felt I was more valuable than what her budget allowed her to pay me. Talk about a mindset of serving those you lead.

Success as a servant-driven leader also requires you to know the importance of one-on-one relationships with the people you lead. I cannot overstress the value of getting to know people at the individual level and hearing their perspectives. The principle of one-on-one meetings is what I used to help a 10,000-person hospital corporation improve its diversity and employee engagement.

When I first arrived, I possessed zero institutional knowledge about the organization or its people, so in my first 100 days, I committed to completing 100 one-on-ones with the different people across the organizational chart. I actually did

141. When I conducted those 141 meetings, I listened before I spoke. I learned a bit about their lives and backgrounds and about their jobs and experiences with the hospital. I wanted to know why they took the jobs they did and what motivated them to stay. I asked them what they thought was best about the organization and where they would like to see change. I listened intently.

People expect a leader to take them to new heights, but they also expect a leader to be connected to the reality of where they have come from. Only at the end did I tell them briefly about myself. The last question I always asked was, "Would you share with me three things you think I could do as a leader to make things better for you?"

A goal for every leader should be to help make the organization and the people within it better every day. To accomplish such a goal and to make certain that those responsible for accomplishing it find meaning and satisfaction in doing so, a leader must be effective at these first twelve actions. Lenora's leadership defined those actions in my life.

PART 2:

Empower them to help Them to Be Successful

Empowerment is the essence of leadership. That means asking, what will I do as a leader to give my team the tools, information, and resources they need to determine their destiny? Here are sixteen ways to build your team up every day.

14 See Their Potential Beyond Their Current Role

Now that you know more about your team members' personal and professional values and goals, you can see where they might excel beyond their current position. For example, maybe they have an aptitude for leadership and can be put on track for a management position. Or perhaps they have a unique skill set that could be an asset to another department.

Before your next round of one-on-one meetings, spend some time thinking about what else each employee could do beyond their current role. Then, talk to them about your ideas to see how you can help them move forward in their careers.

15 Help Them Discover Their Passion

When you get to know someone, you will learn what ignites a fire in them. You may find it's not working for you or your company. That's OK. If their passion lies outside your company, you can help them find it and pursue it. This not only benefits the individual; it also benefits your team. Now you have an open space for someone whose passion aligns with yours.

16 Motivate Them to Achieve Their Goals

The key phrase here is "*their goals.*" Not yours.

People are motivated by different things. Think back to the questions you asked in your one-on-one, especially "what's the best part about your job?" Their answer should give you some clues about what motivates them.

For example, maybe they enjoy the thrill of solving a complex problem for a customer. Or perhaps they love when they get to work with people on other teams. Employees who want collaboration might be motivated to work harder when put on a team with others who rely on them.

Set goals with each team member during your one-on-one meetings, then check in regularly to track their progress and learn what you can do to help them move forward.

17 Teach Them What You Know

Whether you realize it or not, you know many things your team members don't. So, find out where the gaps are and fill them in with knowledge based on your experience.

Some ways to do this include:

- Holding lunch & learns about specific topics
- Offering training sessions to fill in skills gaps
- Sharing your knowledge in the form of a weekly email
- Encourage others to share their expertise so you can all learn from each other
- Leading by example to show instead of telling others how to approach different situations

18 Recognize Their Performance

I've already talked about how important it is for employees to feel seen when they do a good job, no matter how minor the project is. It's equally important to let employees know when their performance is below your expectations. How can they fix something they don't know is broken?

As a leader, you are responsible for letting your team know how they are performing – the good, the bad, and the ugly parts. Then, strategize ways to improve their performance at the team and individual levels.

19 Invest in Their Professional Development

Earlier, I talked about investing in personal growth; however, you should also invest in professional development. If you are a decision-maker in your organization, make room in the budget for training and leadership development. This is the only way you're going to create a team of leaders who will be able to take your company to the next level.

If you're not a decision-maker, then it's up to you to advocate for your team so they can get access to professional development opportunities. Run the numbers to prove the ROI for professional development. Use real-life examples of how your team has succeeded with the help of professional development or suffered because of a lack of it.

Following are examples of the type of training you should pursue for your team:

- Leadership vs. Management
- Fundamentals of Diversity, Equity, & Inclusion
- Strategic Planning
- Succession Planning
- Conducting Performance Evaluations
- Budget Management
- Six Traits of Inclusive Leadership

20 Encourage and Support Philanthropic Endeavors

What better way for your team to get to know each other than by pulling together to serve the community? Encouraging volunteering and community-building activities can help your team work together to solve challenges that will improve their daily lives and the lives of those around them.

The next time you schedule team building, look for a philanthropic endeavor instead of the traditional "drinks after work" routine. Decide what volunteer opportunities to pursue based on your team's interests and values.

21 Get Them the Tools They Need to Be Successful

You wouldn't expect a plumber to show up at your house empty-handed and fix your toilet, would you? Of course not! They need specific tools to do the job.

The same is true for your team, regardless of their job. Ask your team members what they need to be successful. The answers might surprise you. Maybe it's new software, an updated laptop, or a different workspace style.

22 Practice Straightforward, Consistent Communication Every Day

This includes verbal, written, and non-verbal communication. Get to know how your team members like to receive communication. For example, some people prefer email, some like face-to-face, and others prefer a messaging system like Slack.

Whichever model of communication you choose, be purposeful when touching base. Consider hosting weekly informal discussions about what your team is working on and what they need from you to reach their goals. Communicate how each employee fits into the company mission to ensure alignment. In addition, make sure your team hears bad news from you in-person first, not the rumor mill, a company email, or a Zoom meeting. Don't be the CEO or leader who fires people over Zoom.

23 Don't Micromanage

I know. Sometimes, it feels like the only way to get something done is to watch over your employee's shoulder until the task is complete. But that's not doing anybody any favors. Micromanaging implies that you don't trust your team to do what they need to do. It restricts your employees' creativity and innovation by insisting that they do things your way instead of theirs.

Trust your team members to get things done and let them know you are available anytime they have a problem. Instead of obsessing over all the details, set milestones so you can check in on projects at reasonable frequencies.

24 Minimize Fear of the Unknown

People don't like change. It's just a fact of life. Humans have a hard time adapting to change, which is why employees can go into panic mode at the mere whisper of layoffs or reorganization. Give your team as much information as possible as soon as you learn about these rumors or experience layoffs in your organization.

25 Help Them Be Good at Their Life, Not Just Their Job

The best leaders inspire others to become better people, not just better employees. Show up to work every day prepared to lead by example. Be polite to everyone you encounter, from the barista in the lobby café to the CEO. Show everyone the same respect and attention, and watch your culture shift.

26 Be an Advocate for Their Professional Success

You have to be in your employees' corner every single day. Advocate for them to get recognition or a promotion when it's deserved. Push to get them the professional development opportunities that will allow them to grow beyond their current role. Stand up for them, and they will be there for you when you need them.

27 Delegate Important Work, Not Just Tasks

Resist the mentality of "I have to do all the important work." As a leader, you are responsible for training your team to take over some vital work. Trust your team to do more than menial tasks. Monitor them as needed, and let your team know you are available to support them with whatever they need.

28 Sponsor Them

As a leader, you need to act as a sponsor for your team members when they are presented with an opportunity for a promotion. Make a case to the decision-makers as to why this particular team member should be considered and how they will impact the organization for the better with a promotion. Use data to back up your arguments.

29 Be a Mentor, Not Just a Manager

A manager tracks tasks and makes sure work gets done on time. A mentor helps their team grow and develop personally and professionally. When an employee leaves, you won't be their manager anymore. But you can still be their mentor. Holding one-on-one meetings is the best way to build a mentoring relationship with your employees.

CASE STUDY: KATRINA ROCKS

Meet Katrina. She is a passionate and conscientious leader who grew up in a small rural southern town. Before I ever met Katrina in person, I heard about her. I was working for President Obama leading the U.S. Department of Health and Human Services outreach efforts on the Affordable Care Act in the Deep South. I asked my team to survey the states in the southeast for leaders and organizations that were really making an impact on the lives of people. It was then I learned about Katrina's work in Mississippi.

After growing up in a rural community herself, Katrina was passionate about making a difference for underserved people in rural communities. She was leading an effort to help reach people who may be uninsured and underserved as we rolled out the Affordable Care Act. I was impressed that she had the heart to serve people in need. Her efforts weren't perfect, but they were impactful.

It was more than four years later that I would meet Katrina in person. She was now in a different state. She was the Director leading a department of 400 employees inside a $1.6 billion company with 10,000 employees. Katrina was a senior leader with significant budget and financial re-sponsibilities. This was a tougher job than the one she had previously. Her heart to serve wasn't enough to ensure her team thrived. However, Katrina and her team did thrive. Her leadership and team thrived, in part, by making work fun. She was creative in how she motivated and empowered her team.

For one motivational tool, she went outside, literally, and gathered several smooth rocks, which she painted and then wrote the words "You Rock" on them. At the end of the week, she went around the department and gave out rocks to the top performers. She took a photo of each of the recipients, put the photos in a PowerPoint presentation, and emailed it to the whole team. Those who had led success or stepped beyond expectations were recognized. Those who didn't "rock" that week were motivated to be in her slide-show the next month. What could be a simpler motivating tool than a rock?

Katrina also understands the importance of investing in the professional growth and development of her team. Every year, Katrina would host a leadership development training session for her direct reports and each of their direct reports. The session was a day-long session training session focused on leadership skills, communication, empathy, and diversity and inclusion. At the end of the session, she would encourage each team member to put their newly gained skills to use by applying and pursuing new career opportunities within the department and throughout the organization.

Every time I would talk to members of her team, they all were excited to be a part of her team and work in the organization. Her investment in the motivation and empowerment of her team yielded tremendous results not only for her team's performance but her performance as a leader.

For five consecutive years, Katrina received multiple leadership awards for her company for productivity, innovation, and employee engagement. Out of 500 leaders with reported employee engagement scores in the company, Katrina was #8 out of 500. And if based on the size of her employee group, she ranked #1. Again, Katrina rocks! How do you rock as a leader?

PART 3:

Leave a legacy by Showing Them They Can Trust You Forever

Even though you're living in the present, thinking about the future is crucial as you lead your team. You need to focus on what you're going to do to leave your team and the organization better than you found it.

When the time comes for you to leave the organization, whether through promotion, retirement, or a new opportunity, you want to make sure your team is better off because you were there.

Here are fourteen ways to earn your team's trust and respect as a leader as you build your legacy.

30 Be Honest and Ethical

Don't indulge in shady dealings with your colleagues or leadership team. If someone asks you to do something that feels wrong, it probably is. Trust your gut, and always side with what is right and just.

31 Share Your Professional Journey and Personal Story

You didn't get to where you are without making some mistakes along the way. Don't gloss over those! Instead, share your journey and story with your team. When you talk about mistakes, mention how you overcame them or what lessons you learned. This demonstrates that you know how to fix problems and learn from the past.

32 Acknowledge Your Weaknesses, Faults, and Failures

I've seen many leaders make the mistake of thinking they need to be the best at everything. You don't! In fact, you shouldn't be. Part of your job is to find people who excel at particular skills and responsibilities.

Accept responsibility for your faults and failures, then devise an action plan to overcome them. Own up to your mistakes, shortcomings, and limitations, and think about how you react to others. This shows your team members that they are in a safe environment where they can learn and grow.

33 Be Willing to Apologize for Mistakes

After admitting a mistake, apologize for it, especially if it caused undue harm to your team. In addition to saying "I'm sorry," tell your team how you will compensate for it.

For instance, say you let your temper get the best of you during a meeting. Instead of just saying, "I'm sorry I raised my voice yesterday," follow up with some action. "I'm sorry I raised my voice during our meeting yesterday. In the future, when I feel my temper rising, I will step out of the room and take a minute to cool off before coming back to the table to figure out how we can resolve the problem." This lets your team know you are willing to grow and models the behavior you want to see from them in the future.

34 Ask Your Team for Input Regarding Your Areas of Responsibility

Make it a habit to ask for feedback, and encourage all team members to share their viewpoints. Acknowledge your appreciation for their input, especially if their views differ from yours.

35 Create Psychologically Safe Environments

Everyone on your team should know they can speak freely without fearing retaliation. Maybe you're stepping into a leadership role on a team where this wasn't always the case. In that instance, you may need to allow time before your team truly feels free to say what's on their minds.

Holding one-on-one meetings is an excellent way to enable individuals to express themselves without worrying about what other team members will say. And if you do have a team member who wants to retaliate, then it's time to cut them loose.

36 Create Succession Plans for Everyone on Your Team

The days of staying in the same role for 40 years before retirement are over. Today's employees want to know they have chances to grow. That's why you must have a succession plan for every team member. Where do you see each team member in the next one, three, or five years? Spend some time crafting a succession plan for everyone on your team. This should be a unified document to view the collective progress of your team. After you have created the plan, share it with your team so they can see that they have a future with the company.

37 Have Transparent Hiring, Promotion, and Rewards Processes

How do you choose one candidate over another? If you don't have it written down, now is the time to do so. Create an evaluation process that assesses candidates for hiring, promoting, and receiving rewards. It shouldn't be a mystery. If there's no rhyme or reason as to why you hired, promoted, or rewarded one person over another, your team will quickly start mistrusting you and your practices. Let me also underscore that your process and practices could be full of biases even if you believe your process to be objective. For example, I worked with an organization that sought to fill a role with a person with a terminal degree (i.e., Ph.D.)

The job posting stated a terminal degree was required for the role. During the hiring process, several candidates were discussed as less qualified because their terminal degrees were from online for-profit universities rather than traditional education institutions. This was a bias against otherwise highly-qualified candidates who had to work and attend school at the same time rather than take five years out of the workforce to complete their terminal degree. This is wrong and will breed mistrust. Have an unbiased, transparent, and logical process to growth opportunities in your organization.

38 Don't Pretend Your Organization Is Perfect or The Best Place to Work

Your company isn't perfect. Neither is your friend's company that you keep seeing touting their best-place-to-work articles all over your LinkedIn feed. They all have some flaws. That's OK! Instead of acting like your place is the best place in the world to work, acknowledge what those flaws are. Then work with your team and the leadership team to fix them.

You might never reach perfection, but you can get pretty close. First, however, you must also accept that your organization isn't the perfect place for everyone.

39 Show How DEI and Justice Are Essential to Your Company's Success

Whether you have studied DEI intensely or have barely given it a second thought, you need to acknowledge that it is paramount to your organization's success. Everyone in your organization should have a place at the table, regardless of gender, race, socioeconomic status, sexuality, ability, or anything else. Without focusing on diversity, equity, inclusion, and justice, you will never have a world-class workplace culture.

> Without focusing on diversity, equity, inclusion, and justice, you will never have a world-class workplace culture.

40 Do Your Job to Improve Communication, Teamwork, and Culture

If your team's culture isn't healthy, it's your job to fix it. You can't just sit back and say, "well, that's just how things are."

Instead, take actionable steps to improve communication and teamwork. By doing that, you'll improve the culture. So, set up one-on-ones, get in front of your team instead of communicating solely through texts and emails, and point out when someone on your team or elsewhere in the company is being ineffective with their communication.

41 Call People Out for Unethical, Unjust, or Unfair Behavior

You need to adopt a zero-tolerance policy for bad behavior. Call people out when they do and say unscrupulous, unjust, or unethical things, whether a team member or the CEO. Depending on the situation, this may be more effective in a one-on-one conversation than in a public forum. Encourage others to do the same to you without fear of retaliation.

> If your team's culture isn't healthy, it's your job to fix it.

42 Be Visible and Accessible for Your People

Keep an open-door policy if you're in the office so your team knows they can approach you anytime. If you work remotely, you could establish a daily 30-minute team check-in meeting. This meeting can be an open space for everyone on the team to log on and say hello. The ultimate goal is to ensure you are easy to reach by email, text, messaging application, or video conferencing services.

43 Celebrate Team Successes and Individual Improvement

Your team's success is your success. It can be as big as finishing a significant project ahead of the deadline or as small as getting everyone to a meeting on time. Whatever it is, take the time to notice and celebrate improvements, big and small.

44 Be a Role Model for Fairness, Respect, and Inclusion

Lead by example in everything you do. Let your team and other company leaders see that you are a champion for justice, respect, and inclusion through your actions. Find ways to demonstrate this every single day.

CASE STUDY: WALSH'S WAY

You may not understand the details of American professional football, but almost everyone who knows pro football is familiar with the name Bill Walsh. Bill Walsh was a legendary college and professional football coach who is known for creating a play-calling system called The West Coast Offense. This system was radically different from anything before or after it was created.

Using this system, Walsh's record was 102–63–1 (wins-losses-ties) with the San Francisco 49ers, winning ten of his fourteen postseason games along with six division titles, three NFC Championship titles, and three Super Bowls. He was named NFL Coach of the Year in 1981 and 1984. In

1993, he was elected to the Pro Football Hall of Fame. At first blush, you would think the West Coast Offense and success as a pro coach is Walsh's greatest legacy. It's not.

After landing his first and only NFL head coaching job in 1979, Bill Walsh knew that success on the field required the best coaches. However, the National Football League wasn't a place where the best black and other minority coaches were given opportunities to demonstrate their coaching ability. Bill Walsh sought to change that. After seeking counsel, input, and mentorship from a renowned African American Sports Sociologist, Harry Edwards, Walsh became an aggressive advocate for the recruitment, retention, and promotion of black men into NFL coaching.

In 1983, he hired his first two African American assistant coaches. Within three years, he hired three more black men as assistants. For all five black men, this was their first job in the National Football League. Two of the five would later become NFL head coaches. Not only was Walsh an example of fairness, respect, and inclusion, but he also became a champion for diversity across the NFL. All of these minority men grew to trust Walsh's leadership. They saw him challenge NFL owners and management staff to give his current and former minority assistants opportunities to be head coaches. He would repeatedly state that diversity in NFL coaching would be critical to the success of pro football, given that 70% of its players are racially and ethnically diverse.

In the summer of 1987, in his final season as the 49ers' head coach, Walsh would solidify his legacy when he brought in Marvin Lewis, an African American college coach, for an internship. This first summer internship from a legendary successful pro football coach would become a transparent pathway for many more minorities to become coaches in the National Football League.

The Bill Walsh Minority Coaching fellowship has lasted for more than thirty-five years, providing talented minority coaches the opportunity to work alongside the NFL staff and expose them to NFL practice methods, training techniques, and offensive and defensive philosophies. Graduates of the program receive formal evaluations and letters of recommendation.

Since its inception, the program has trained and mentored more than 2,000 diverse coaches, and now every NFL team participates in the program.

With recent news headlines, the NFL is still struggling to maintain racial diversity at the head coaching level. However, if you look back at how many African American men have ever been permanent head coaches in the national football league, more than 50% of them (thirteen in total) can trace their lineage to Bill Walsh. This is what legacy looks like.

CHALLENGING YOURSELF TO BECOME A WORLD-CLASS LEADER

Think about some of the most outstanding leaders in business, society, government, and the world. The ones we remember, like Nelson Mandela, Martin Luther King, Jr., Mother Teresa, Gandhi, Jesus, and even Oprah.

Why do we all know precisely who these people are? Because they have a legacy built on their beliefs, behaviors, and actions. They have a legacy sharing a commitment to justice through their actions. Great leaders like the ones mentioned above:

- Despise unfairness and injustice
- Do something every day to make the world more just and fair
- Got comfortable being uncomfortable
- Value diversity, equity, and inclusion
- Work with others to make change

- Don't quit when things get hard
- Take a long-term approach to solving problems
- Don't make excuses
- Take responsibility when things go wrong
- Share responsibility when things go right

The 100-Day Challenge to Just Lead: Serve, Empower, and Leave a Lasting Legacy

I hope you're fired up and ready to Just Lead. Putting all 44 actions into practice is the most important thing you can do to build a great organization and become the leader that everyone admires. However, I realize that figuring out where to start can feel daunting. That's why I've created the 100-day challenge to help you focus on your personal growth so you can become a better leader for everyone around you.

Even if you feel that you are a successful and impactful leader today, you have to keep growing. What got you to where you are today won't keep you there tomorrow. It surely won't get you to the next level. Instead, you must continue to develop yourself as a leader to face tomorrow's challenges.

With that in mind, I am challenging you to spend the next 100 days taking action on each aspect of leadership: service, empowerment, and leaving a legacy. I have outlined a simple framework to help you get started on the next phase of your leadership journey. I also want to invite you to share your progress with other leaders who have committed themselves to using these action steps to break down, boost your retention and build a world-class culture. Join our JUST LEAD Group on LinkedIn.

30 Days of Service

Over the next thirty days, perform one random act of service for your employees and colleagues each day. To help you develop some ideas for how to do this, use the five one-on-one questions that I gave you in Action Step #2 to get to know your team.

1 Day of Reflection

After thirty days of random acts of service, take some time to write down what you have learned about yourself over the previous thirty days. How did you make a difference in the lives of others? Where did you make the most significant impact? Which acts of service will you repeat in the future and why?

30 Days of Empowerment

Make a daily practice of inspiring and empowering those you lead. You can do this in several ways, including:

- Providing compliments
- Providing motivational words
- Giving positive encouragement
- Sharing your experiences and advice
- Saying affirmations related to their professional growth

1 Day of Reflection

After focusing on empowerment for thirty days, write down how others responded to your actions. Where did you see noticeable growth? Did you notice a change in your team's mood throughout the thirty-day period? What steps will you implement in the future and why?

30 Days of Legacy

Before starting these final thirty days, identify three people who could feasibly succeed you in your role. Then, spend this month meeting with and mentoring them. Share your insights and experiences with them, so they can be more prepared to step up into a leadership position in the future.

1 Day of Reflection

Imagine yourself reaching the end of your prosperous professional career. What do you want to be remembered for? How would you share this information with first-time managers? Write down what you want them to know so they can be better prepared than you were.

Visualization

After your final reflection, spend three days focusing on the following question: If you had unlimited money, time, and support from family and friends, what would you do for the rest of your life? Then, think about what you will be doing twenty years from now. Where do you see your future headed?

Celebration

You have reached the end of the challenge and deserve to be rewarded for all your effort. Remember, it's good to be good to yourself! Serving, empowering others, and building a legacy are all big-picture ideas. However, it's important to celebrate all the little wins and hard work that happens in between the big moments.

Being a great leader should build you up, not drag you down. So, take these final four days to celebrate personal, professional, and team wins, no matter how big or small.

It takes a lot of work to lead. However, the best leaders never quit learning.

Final Thoughts

Being a leader isn't easy, and it isn't for the weak. If you have ever thought you couldn't lead because you aren't a "born leader," I have news for you – nobody is! It takes a lot of work to lead. However, the best leaders never quit learning how to develop themselves to take their professions and teams to the next level.

When it comes to addressing the increasingly complex modern societal challenges, we need leaders willing to take their successes from the workplace into society. We need leaders willing to strengthen American democracy. This is the leadership we need this from you.

I'd encourage you to reflect on your leadership style and find ways to implement all 44 action steps. Then, your team, organization, and America will thank you.

References

2022 workplace DEI report. Culture Amp. (2022, January 25). Retrieved June 20, 2022, from https://www.cultureamp.com/workplace-dei-report-2022

Abramson, A. (2022, January 1). *Burnout and stress are everywhere*. Monitor on Psychology. Retrieved June 20, 2022, from https://www.apa.org/monitor/2022/01/special-burnout-stress

CG-great-resigners-research-report-FINAL.pdf. Cengage Group. (2022, January). Retrieved June 20, 2022, from https://cengage.widen.net/s/78hrkqgfj7/cg-great-resigners-research-report-final

Employee engagement statistics 2022: Increased productivity? TeamStage. (2022, January 21). Retrieved June 20, 2022, from https://teamstage.io/employee-engagement-statistics/

Hrala, J. (2021, November 8). *The H.R. News Wire: Toxic Cultures have cost companies $223 billion over the last 5 years*. The H.R. News Wire: Toxic Cultures Have Cost Companies $223 Billion Over the Last 5 Years. Retrieved June 20, 2022, from https://blog.careerminds.com/community/toxic-cultures-have-cost-companies-223-billion

Ladika, S. (2021, July 31). *Trust has never been more important*. SHRM. Retrieved June 20, 2022, from https://www.shrm.org/hr-today/news/all-things-work/pages/trust-has-never-been-more-important.aspx

McFeely, S., & Wigert, B. (2022, June 10). *This fixable problem costs U.S. businesses $1 trillion*. Gallup.com. Retrieved June 20, 2022, from https://www.gallup.com/workplace/247391/fixable-problem-costs-businesses-trillion.aspx

Parker, K., & Horowitz, J. M. (2022, March 10). *The majority of workers who quit a job in 2021 cite low pay, no opportunities for advancement, feeling disrespected*. Pew Research Center. Retrieved June 20, 2022, from https://www.pewresearch.org/fact-tank/2022/03/09/majority-of-workers-who-quit-a-job-in-2021-cite-low-pay-no-opportunities-for-advancement-feeling-disrespected

Patel, K. (2022, April 15). *Gauging the impact of the great resignation*. Evive. Retrieved June 20, 2022, from https://goe-vive.com/gauging-the-impact-of-the-great-resignation/

The state of internal mobility and employee retention report. Lever. (2022, February 3). Retrieved June 20, 2022, from https://www.lever.co/research/2022-internal-mobility-and-employee-retention-report/

Sull, D., Sull, C., & Zweig, B. (2022, January 11). *Toxic culture is driving the great resignation.* MIT Sloan Management Review. Retrieved June 20, 2022, from https://sloanreview.mit.edu/article/toxic-culture-is-driving-the-great-resignation/

Workplace Burnout Survey: Deloitte U.S. Deloitte United States. (2020, April 24). Retrieved June 20, 2022, from https://www2.deloitte.com/us/en/pages/about-deloitte/articles/burnout-survey.html

Zak, P. J. (2021, August 31). *The Neuroscience of Trust.* Harvard Business Review. Retrieved June 20, 2022, from https://hbr.org/2017/01/the-neuroscience-of-trust

Social Security Fact Sheet. Social Security Administration. (n.d.). Retrieved June 20, 2022, from https://www.ssa.gov/pressoffice/IncRetAge.html

Connect with Anton

I am grateful that you have taken the time to read this book. I hope that it has been helpful to you. I would love to hear from you about how you have applied the principles in this book. Please get in touch with me in the following ways:

- See my quotes, videos, and photos on Instagram @ antonjgunn
- Read automated posts and impromptu rants on Twitter @antonjgunn
- Connect for business content on LinkedIn https://www.linkedin.com/in/antonjgunn/

Gain free training resources on my YouTube page: https://www.youtube.com/antonjgunn

If you would like to help spread this message or continue the conversation with leaders in any organization, here are five ways you can help:

1. Leave an honest rating/review wherever you purchased this book.
2. Share a picture of this book on Instagram, Twitter, Facebook, and/or LinkedIn (please tag me at @antonjgunn or the hashtag #JustLead).
3. Gift a copy to a friend/colleague.
4. Organize a formal group book read with your organization.
5. Most importantly, if you're looking to hire a dynamic, engaging speaker for your next event or need a leadership expert who can help you create a world-class culture in your organization using these principles, visit www.antongunn.com or email me directly at anton@antongunn.com.

Other books by Anton J. Gunn

*The Audacity of Leadership: 10 Essentials to Becoming a
Transformative Leader in the 21st Century*

*The Presidential Principles: How to Inspire Action
and Create Lasting Impact*

www.ingramcontent.com/pod-product-compliance
Lightning Source LLC
Chambersburg PA
CBHW060241030426
42335CB00014B/1565